A Kid's Guide to Drawing America™

How to Draw
Tennessee's
Sights and Symbols

Melody S. Mis

The Rosen Publishing Group's
PowerKids Press™
New York

To friends and family, who encouraged me to write

Published in 2002 by The Rosen Publishing Group, Inc.
29 East 21st Street, New York, NY 10010

First Edition

Project Editor: Jannell Khu
Book Design: Kim Sonsky
Layout Design: Michael Donnellan

Illustration Credits: Emily Muschinske
Photo Credits: pp. 7, 22 © Bettmann/CORBIS; p. 8 (photo) © McClung Historical Collection; p. 8 (sketch) Special Collections at the University of Tennessee; p. 9 (painting) © Collection of the Greenville County Museum of Art, purchased with funds donated by Dorothy Hipp Gunter; pp. 12, 14 © One Mile Up, Incorporated; p. 16 © Pat O'Hara/CORBIS; p. 18 © Lee Snider; Lee Snider/CORBIS; p. 20 © Steve Kaufman/CORBIS; p. 24 © Philip Gould/CORBIS; p. 26 © Dave G. Houser/CORBIS; p. 28 © Raymond Gehman/CORBIS.

Mis, Melody S., 1965–
How to draw Tennessee's sights and symbols / Melody S. Mis.
p. cm. — (A kid's guide to drawing America)
Includes index.
Summary: This book explains how to draw some of Tennessee's sights and symbols, including the state seal, the official flower, and Nashville's Union Station.
   ISBN 0-8239-6099-4
1. Emblems, State—Tennessee—Juvenile literature 2. Tennessee—In art—Juvenile literature 3. Drawing—Technique—Juvenile literature [1. Emblems, State— Tennessee 2. Tennessee
3. Drawing—Technique] I. Title II. Series
   743'.8'99768—dc21

Manufactured in the United States of America

CONTENTS

Let's Draw Tennessee

There are many museums and historical places to visit in Tennessee. The National Civil Rights Museum in Memphis traces the events of the Civil Rights movement of the 1950s and the 1960s. Before the movement, African Americans received unequal treatment in the United States. For instance African American children had to attend separate schools that were inferior to the schools that white children attended. Americans of all races protested this kind of practice and worked to get equal rights for African Americans and other minorities.

You can also visit historical homes of U.S. presidents James K. Polk, Andrew Johnson, and Andrew Jackson. Today their homes are preserved as museums. The most famous is The Hermitage in Nashville. It belonged to Andrew Jackson.

Nashville is famous for its music industry. Exhibits at the Country Music Hall of Fame in Nashville trace the city's musical history. Many famous musical performers are native to Tennessee. The Queen of Soul, Aretha Franklin, was born in Memphis. Rock-and-roll singer Tina Turner was born in Nutbush. Country singer Dolly

Parton was born in Sevierville. You can visit Dolly's theme park, Dollywood, in Pigeon Forge, Tennessee! The blues got their start in Memphis. They were created by southern African American musicians such as Tennessee native W. C. Handy. Handy is called the Father of Blues. In Memphis you can visit Graceland, where rock-and-roll singer Elvis Presley lived. This book shows you how to draw some of Tennessee's sights and symbols. You start with one shape and add other shapes to it. New shapes are shown in red. Directions are printed under each step. Before you start, gather the following supplies:

- A sketch pad
- An eraser
- A number 2 pencil
- A pencil sharpener

These are some of the shapes and drawing terms you need to know to draw Tennessee's sights and symbols:

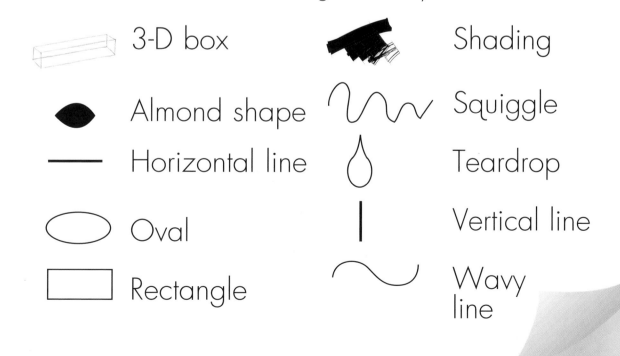

3-D box

Almond shape

Horizontal line

Oval

Rectangle

Shading

Squiggle

Teardrop

Vertical line

Wavy line

The Volunteer State

Tennessee is nicknamed the Volunteer State, because many men from Tennessee volunteered to fight against the British in the War of 1812. Tennessee is also called the Mother of Southern Statesmen. Three U.S. presidents were born in North Carolina but made Tennessee their home when they were young men. These men, James K. Polk, Andrew Johnson, and Andrew Jackson, served in Tennessee's legislature before they served as U.S. presidents.

Tennessee's capital, Nashville, has a famous nickname, Music City USA. Nashville has the biggest country music industry in the world. Nashville's music industry began with the Grand Ole Opry. The Grand Ole Opry is a country music show that has been broadcasted on the radio since 1925.

The University of Tennessee's women's basketball team is called the Lady Volunteers! Tennessee is proud of the team's coach, Pat Head Summitt. She is a native of Henrietta, Tennessee. Summitt was inducted into the Women's Basketball Hall of Fame in 1999.

Andrew Jackson (1767–1845) was the seventh president of the United States, from 1829 to 1837. Jackson was a major general in the War of 1812 and became a national hero when he defeated the British at New Orleans, Louisiana.

Tennessee Artist

Catherine Wiley

Catherine Wiley (1879–1958) was born near Knoxville, Tennessee. She studied art at the University of Tennessee. In 1903, Wiley went to New York and studied at the Art Students League. While there Wiley was exposed to American impressionism. This was when Wiley started to paint in the impressionist style.

Impressionism developed in France during the nineteenth century. Impressionist artists recorded the way light and colors affected their subject matter. They often used unmixed paint colors and rough brushstrokes to capture the colors of nature. For example, to paint grass, an artist might have brushed a streak of blue

Wiley was a gifted illustrator. She sketched this picture with pencil on paper. 8¾ x 11¾ inches (22 x 30 cm).

and a streak of yellow paint next to each other. From a distance, the blue and yellow colors would seem to blend to make the grass look bright green.

Take a look at *A Sunlit Afternoon.* Most people think of light, bright colors when they think of a sunny afternoon. Although the painting is a scene of people, what takes center stage is the contrast between light and dark colors. The brightness of the people's clothes jump out against the dark wooded area. The grass and tree leaves look yellowish green in the areas where they are sunlit and nearly black where they are not. With this painting Wiley shows us that a sunny afternoon can be light and dark at the same time.

Wiley painted *A Sunlit Afternoon* around 1915. It was done in oil on canvas and measures 36" x 40" (91 cm x 124 cm). In the lower part of the painting, notice the brushstrokes. Wiley purposely used rough brushstrokes to paint the grass.

Map of Tennessee

Map of the Continental United States

Eastern Tennessee includes the Appalachian and Great Smoky Mountains. The Great Smoky Mountains got their name from the blue mist that makes the mountains look smoky. In this area is Clingmans Dome. At 6,643 feet (2,025 m) tall, it is the state's tallest mountain. Tennessee's middle region is where vegetables are produced and livestock are raised. Between the Tennessee and Mississippi Rivers lies western Tennessee. Historians say the New Madrid earthquakes of 1811–1812 caused the Mississippi River to flow backward for three days! This caused the river to flood a huge crack, also caused by the earthquake, and to form Reelfoot Lake. Reelfoot Lake is famous for its bald eagle population.

1

Draw a long, thin rectangle. This shape is only a guide to help you draw in the shape of Tennessee.

2

Draw two slanted vertical lines inside the rectangle. Notice that the right line slants more than the left line.

3

Next draw a horizontal line that slants slightly upward.

4

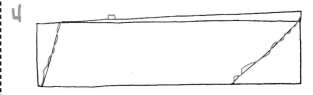

Draw the eastern and western borders of Tennessee with wavy lines. Add the tiny rectangular piece of land that sticks out of the northwestern part of the state.

5

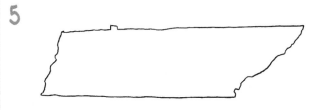

Erase extra lines so that your state looks like the above.

♠	Cherokee National Forest
⋀⋀	Great Smoky Mountains National Park
◉	Memphis
✪	Nashville
⟍	Ocoee River

6

Add some of Tennessee's key places:
a. Draw three tree shapes for Cherokee National Forest
b. Draw several pointed shapes for Great Smoky Mountains National Park
c. Add a line for Ocoee River.
d. For Nashville, the state's capital, draw a circle around a star.
e. Draw a circle around a dot for Memphis.

The State Seal

Tennessee has had a seal since 1796. However, the state did not officially adopt the current seal until 1987. The seal used today is very similar to the seal used in 1796. On the seal is the year, 1796, which is the when Tennessee became a state. In the middle of the seal is the word "agriculture." A plow, a bundle of wheat, and a cotton plant are shown to symbolize Tennessee's agriculture. On top of the bundle of wheat is the Roman numeral XVI. This stands for when Tennessee became the sixteenth state to be admitted to the Union. On the bottom center of the seal is the word "commerce," which means trade. Above this word a riverboat floats on a body of

water. The boat represents transportation and trade.

1

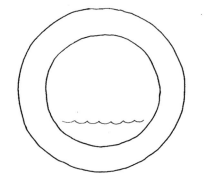

Draw two circles and a wavy line for the water.

2

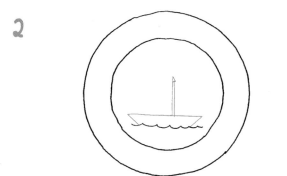

Add the bottom of the ship and a pole, or mast.

3

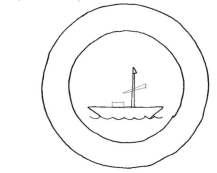

Add the cross bar on the mast and a rectangle on top of the boat.

4

Above the boat draw the bundle of wheat and the cotton plant.

5

Draw a plow next to the bundle of wheat.

6

Write "THE GREAT SEAL OF THE STATE OF TENNESSEE 1796." Notice the two stars on either side of 1796. Inside the smaller circle, write "XVI," "AGRICULTURE," and "COMMERCE."

7

Add all the details you see. Shade the seal, and you're done!

The State Flag

Tennessee's state flag was adopted in 1905. It was designed by Captain LeRoy Reeves. He was a member of the Tennessee infantry. The flag is red, white, and blue, the same colors as those of the nation's flag. The flag has a red background with a white circle in the center. The circle symbolizes the unity of the eastern, middle, and western regions of Tennessee. Inside the circle are three white stars on a blue background. According to Reeves, the stars represent the three regions of Tennessee. A blue stripe is on the right edge of the flag. Next to the blue stripe is a narrow white stripe. Reeves added these stripes to break up the bright red background.

1

Draw a rectangle.

2

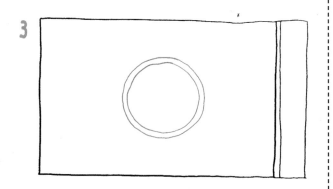

Draw two vertical parallel lines on the right side of the rectangle.

3

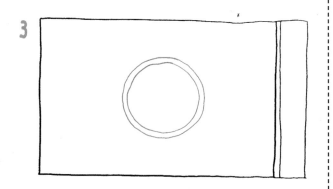

In the center of the rectangle, draw two circles, one inside the other.

4

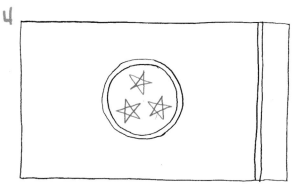

Add three stars inside the circles.

5

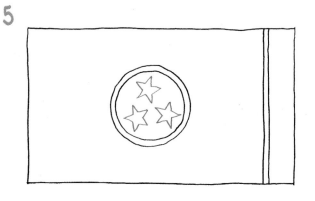

Erase the extra lines in the stars so that your stars are solid white. You're done!

15

The Iris

Tennessee adopted the purple iris as the state flower in 1933. It has three petals that symbolize wisdom, faith, and bravery. The size of the petals can vary from 1 inch (2.5 cm) to 12 inches (30 cm). The iris grows well in the moist, well-drained soil of the Tennessee woodlands.

The iris comes in almost all colors of the rainbow. In Greek mythology, Iris was the goddess of the rainbow and the messenger of the gods. Her name means "eye of heaven." The colored part of your eye is called the iris. In ancient civilizations, the iris flower was used to make medicines that treated headaches, colds, snakebites, and sunburn. It was also used to make perfume. Today the iris is used to make cosmetics.

1

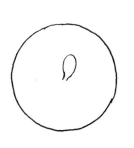

Draw a circle. This will be your guide as you draw the iris. Next add the tiny petal in the middle of the circle. It should be oval shaped with an opening in the bottom.

2

Draw another oval-shaped, little petal to the left of the first one you drew. Now they look like two rabbit ears!

3

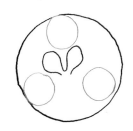

Draw three circles. These are your guides for drawing the three large petals of the iris.

4

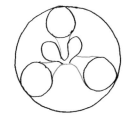

Connect the circles to the two small petals that look like rabbit ears.

5

After you erase extra lines, your drawing should look like the above. Notice that the three circles you drew in step 3 now look like lightbulbs. For the flower stem, add two long vertical parallel lines.

6

You are ready to shade. Leave some of the areas in the petal white. Good job!

The Tulip Tree

The tulip tree (*Liriodendron tulipifera*) is also called the tulip poplar. It was adopted as Tennessee's state tree in 1947. It was chosen because Tennessee pioneers used the wood from the tulip tree to build their houses and barns. Native Americans made canoes from the trunk of the tulip tree.

The tulip tree can grow to be 200 feet (61 m) high. The flower of the tulip tree blooms in spring. It has greenish yellow petals that form a cup. The cup looks like the garden flower we know as the tulip.

The cup is 2 inches (5 cm) across and has an orange center. The tulip tree can be found in the eastern half of the United States. It thrives in well-drained soil. The tulip tree's lumber is used to make furniture and toys. Its seeds provide food for birds, squirrels, and other animals.

1

First draw a slightly curved vertical line. This is the tree's right side line. Next draw the lines to the tree's left side. Notice that the trunk splits into two branches at the top.

2

Continue the branch that reaches straight up. To this branch, add a smaller branch that forks to the right.

3

Draw a branch that shoots off to the upper left. Finish drawing the branch below the one you just drew. Now the tree has four large branches.

4

Draw a lot of thin branches that grow from the four large branches. The more branches you draw, the fuller your tree will look!

5

Draw the outline of the tree's leafy areas.

6

Shade the tree, and you are done!

The Mockingbird

The mockingbird became Tennessee's state bird in 1933. Mockingbirds live in the nation's southeastern states. Tennessee's forests, valleys, and gardens make ideal homes for the mockingbird. The top of a mockingbird's body is grayish brown, and its belly is white. Its tail is long and grayish black. Mockingbirds measure from 9 to 11 inches (23–28 cm) long. Although small, these birds aren't afraid to defend themselves. They use their sharp beaks to peck their enemies.

The mockingbird is one of the best singers among birds. The mockingbird can imitate the songs of other birds in its environment. It can even imitate barking dogs! No wonder the Native Americans called the mockingbird the bird of 400 tongues.

1

Begin with an oval for the body.

2

Add a circle for the head. The circle should slightly overlap the body.

3

Draw a straight line and a curved line to form the tail feather.

4

Draw the left leg and the beginning of the other leg. Add a beak to the head.

5

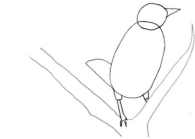

Draw the bird's perch. The perch is a *V*-shaped branch.

6

Draw the wings. The two wings are different in size and shape. Next draw its eye.

7

Use curved lines to shape the bottom parts of the wings. Fill in the eye. Erase extra lines.

8

Finish adding details, and shade your bird. Notice the light and dark areas of the chest and wing.

Elvis Presley and Graceland

Elvis Presley was born in Mississippi in 1935. His family moved to Memphis, Tennessee, in 1948. Elvis is called the King of Rock and Roll. He combined the sounds of blues, gospel, and country music to create a new style of music called rock and roll. Many of the songs Elvis recorded in the 1950s are considered classics and are still very popular today.

In 1957, Elvis bought a mansion in Memphis called Graceland. Elvis lived there off and on until his death in 1977. He is buried in the Meditation Garden at Graceland. Today Elvis's home, gardens, and collections are open to the public. Visitors can see the rooms where Elvis lived. Elvis's gold records, awards, and stage costumes are displayed in the Trophy Room.

1

Begin with a long oval. Next add a small rectangle underneath the oval. This is the microphone.

2

Add a *U*-shaped line under the oval. Next draw two long, vertical parallel lines.

3

Look at the photo of Elvis on page 22. Study the basic shapes that make up his head and body. Elvis's head is an oval that is wider at the top. The shape of the jacket is shaped like a rectangle. Draw the rectangle at a slight slant to the right. Nice job.

4

Draw the outline of his hair. Then add the basic shapes of his arms. These shapes will be your guides as you add more details.

5

Follow the red lines above to add details to Elvis's clothes. It is easier if you work from the top to the bottom, one line at a time.

6

Use the arm guides you drew in step 4 to draw in the details. Notice that both arms are bent, but in different ways. Erase extra lines.

7

Draw Elvis's face. He is looking down so you can't see all of his eyes. His mouth is open because he is singing. Draw details on his left arm.

8

Add the final details to Elvis's jacket. Shade your drawing, and you're done!

The Music Jukebox

The jukebox got its name from the southern African American word *jook*, which means "to dance." A jukebox is a coin-operated machine that plays songs. The jukebox has a list of songs. After a person puts a coin into the coin slot, he or she pushes the button next to the song he or she wants to hear. This causes the machine to play that song. The jukebox provided entertainment for guests at dance halls and other gathering places.

The jukebox was especially important for Memphis musicians who recorded the blues. It was the only way that many Americans could hear the blues. During the early 1900s, the radio played orchestral music, so fans of the blues turned to the jukebox to hear this new kind of music. Also, many people could not afford radios during the early 1900s, but most could afford a nickel to play their favorite songs on the jukebox!

24

1

Toward the bottom of your paper, draw a straight line that slants slightly upward. Draw a curved dome shape from one end of the line and connect it to the other end.

2

Inside the shape you just drew, draw a smaller version of that shape. Next draw the three shapes shown above.

3

Add two curved lines on the top left side and do the same for the right side. Fill the two rectangular boxes with small horizontal lines.

4

Draw two parallel lines between the striped rectangles. Under these two lines, draw a small rectangle. On the right side, draw an *L*. Next draw a flipped *L* on the left side.

5

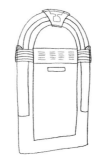

Inside the long rectangle, draw small horizontal lines. These are the list of songs. Add the other details shown in red in this step.

6

Next draw another *U* shape. Add six lines inside the *U* shape. Draw a small circle and put a star in the middle of the circle.

7

Draw lines that crisscross each other. This is the jukebox speaker.

8

Shade your jukebox, and you're done!

25

Nashville's Union Station

The Louisville and Nashville (L & N) Railroad Company started construction on Nashville's Union Station in 1898. The station was completed in 1900. The station was designed in the Romanesque style. This style of architecture uses round arches, towers, and vaulted ceilings. A clock tower was built at one end of the building. On top of the clock tower stands a statue of Mercury, the Roman god of trade. Along the lobby walls, bas-relief panels show the history of transportation. Bas-relief is a process of carving figures that stick out from the background. Also in the lobby are angel sculptures holding symbols that represent Tennessee products, such as corn and livestock. In 1986, Union Station was converted into a hotel.

1

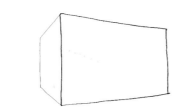

Begin with a slanted rectangle. The left vertical line is longer than the right vertical line. The top horizontal line slants downward and the bottom line slants upward.

2

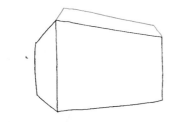

Add three lines on the left side of the rectangle you just drew. Again, notice the direction in which the horizontal lines slant. You just drew a 3-D box.

3

Add the roof. It is made with two short, slanted vertical lines connected by a long horizontal line.

4

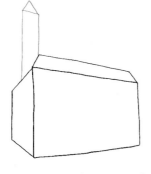

Add the tower on the top left side of the building. Draw a triangle on top.

5

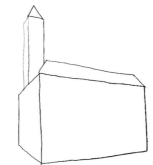

Add the side of the tower.

6

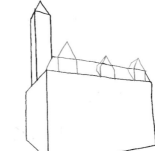

Next draw three dormers. Dormers are small areas that stick out of the roof. They are made with triangle shapes. Study the drawing above before you start.

7

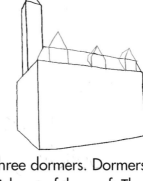

Add the little tower behind the center dormer. Draw triangular shapes behind the first and the last dormer. Divide the front of the building into three sections.

8

Add the windows, and shade. Good job!

Tennessee's Capitol

Tennessee's capitol was built between 1845 and 1855. Architect William Strickland designed the capitol in the Greek Ionic style. Ionic is a style of architecture that became popular after 500 B.C. One feature of Ionic architecture requires the use of slender, fluted columns. A fluted column is like a tall, thick pole that has grooves, or long cuts, down the sides. At the top of each column is a carved piece of stonework. It connects the column to an arch or to a wooden beam. There are 14 columns on the outside of the capitol. There are also statues of famous men, including President Andrew Jackson, who made Tennessee their home. President James K. Polk is buried on the capitol's grounds.

1

Draw a rectangle. Notice that the top horizontal line slants noticeably upward. Also, notice that the left vertical line is much shorter than the right vertical line.

2

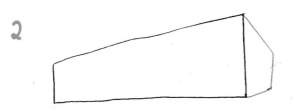

Add another slanted rectangle on the right side of the first one. You have made a 3-D box.

3

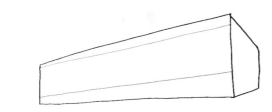

Draw two lines across the front of the building to break it into three sections.

4

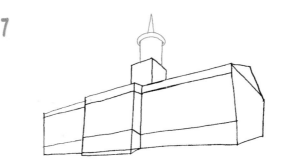

On the right side, draw two short, slanted lines that meet in a point.

5

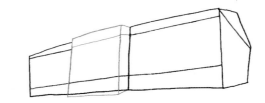

Next draw the part of the building that comes forward.

6

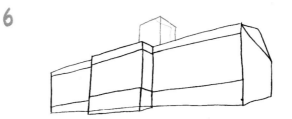

Add the base of the tower on the top of the building. It is made by drawing two slanted rectangles right next to each other.

7

Next add the tower. Draw two vertical lines. Add two curved lines, and top it off with a narrow triangle.

8

Add the windows and columns. Shade your capitol building. You can add a tree in the right corner.

Tennessee State Facts

Statehood	June 1, 1796, 16th state
Area	42,144 square miles (109,152 sq km)
Population	5,483,500
Capital	Nashville, population, 511,263
Most Populated City	Memphis, population, 596,725
Industries	Chemicals, textiles, machinery, music, automobiles, furniture
Agriculture	Tobacco, corn, cotton, soybeans, livestock
Nickname	The Volunteer State
Motto	Agriculture And Commerce
Tree	Tulip poplar
Flower	Iris
Bird	Mockingbird
Insects	Firefly, ladybug, and honeybee
Animal	Raccoon
Horse	Tennessee walking horse
Fish	Channel catfish
Butterfly	Zebra swallowtail
Song	"My Homeland Tennessee"
Gem	Tennessee pearl
Reptile	Eastern box turtle
Rock	Limestone

Glossary

blues (BLOOZ) Sad songs that came from religious songs.

civilizations (sih-vuh-luh-ZAY-shunz) Groups of people that have reached an advanced state of social organization, technology, and culture.

classics (KLA-siks) Things that keep their popularity for a long time.

environment (en-VY-urn-ment) All the living things and conditions that make up a place.

gospel (GOS-puhl) Religious, pertaining to the Bible.

Greek mythology (GREEK mih-THAH-luh-jee) Stories that people from Greece believed in during ancient times.

Hall of Fame (HAWL UV FAYM) A group of individuals who have been selected and recognized for their success.

imitate (IH-muh-tayt) To copy someone or something.

inducted (in-DUKT-ed) Made a part of something.

infantry (IN-fuhn-tree) A group of people in the military.

inferior (in-FEER-ee-ur) Of poor quality or below average.

minorities (my-NOR-ih-teez) The smaller parts of a group or a whole.

pioneers (py-uh-NEERZ) Some of the first people to settle in a new area.

preserved (prih-ZURVD) To have kept something from being lost or destroyed.

vaulted ceilings (VAWLT-ed SEE-lingz) Arched ceilings made of stone or concrete.

Index

Web Sites

To learn more about Tennessee, check out these Web sites:
http://greatsmokymountains.areaparks.com/parkinformation.html?content=kids
http://home.digitalcity.com/memphis/visitorsguide
　　www.halloffame.org
　www.tennesseehistory.com